SHAKESPEARE: RICHARD III

by

D.C. GUNBY

Professor of English,
The University of Canterbury,
New Zealand

EDWARD ARNOLD

© D.C. Gunby 1980

First published 1980 by
Edward Arnold (Publishers) Ltd
41 Bedford Square, London WC1B 3DQ

British Library Cataloguing in Publication Data

Gunby, David Charles
  Shakespeare, 'Richard III'. — (Studies in
English literature; 71).
  1. Shakespeare, William. Richard III
  I. Title   II. Series
  822.3'3   PR2821

  ISBN 0 7131 6284 8 Pbk

Printed in Great Britain by
The Camelot Press Ltd,
Southampton

rvull 1981

STUDIES IN ENGLISH LITERATURE No. 71

General Editor

David Daiches

Already published in the series:

Already published in the series (*continued*):

General Preface

The object of this series is to provide studies of individual novels, plays and groups of poems and essays which are known to be widely read by students. The emphasis is on clarification and evaluation; biographical and historical facts, while they may be discussed when they throw light on particular elements in a writer's work, are generally subordinated to critical discussion. What kind of work is this? What exactly goes on here? How good is this work, and why? These are the questions that each writer will try to answer.

It should be emphasized that these studies are written on the assumption that the reader has already read carefully the work discussed. The objective is not to enable students to deliver opinions about works they have not read, nor is it to provide ready-made ideas to be applied to works that have been read. In one sense all critical interpretation can be regarded as foisting opinions on readers, but to accept this is to deny the advantages of any sort of critical discussion directed at students or indeed at anybody else. The aim of these studies is to provide what Coleridge called in another context 'aids to reflection' about the works discussed. The interpretations are offered as suggestive rather than as definitive, in the hope of stimulating the reader into developing further his own insights. This is after all the function of all critical discourse among sensible people.

Because of the interest which this kind of study has aroused, it has been decided to extend it first from merely English literature to include also some selected works of American literature and now further to include selected works in English by Commonwealth writers. The criterion will remain that the book studied is important in itself and is widely read by students.

DAVID DAICHES

Contents

1. Introduction

The three parts of *Henry VI*, so far as is known Shakespeare's first dramatic work, brought the unknown and (in the eyes of the established university-trained writers like Nashe, Peele, and Greene) uneducated provincial to modest public notice, and drew from the dying Greene, alarmed at the prospect of mere actors usurping the dramatist's rôle, the famous punning reference to

> an vpstart Crow, beautified with our feathers, that with his *Tygers hart wrapt in a Players hyde*, supposes he is as well able to bombast out a blanke verse as the best of you: an beeing and absolute *Iohannes fac totum*, is in his owne conceit the onely Shake-scene in a countrey.[1]

Greene died early in September 1592, the month in which his attack on Shakespeare appeared in *Greene's Groats-worth of Wit*. By then, it may well be, Shakespeare was already working on his fourth play, one which, by its great and immediate success, would have alarmed Greene much more than *Henry VI*. In the event, Shakespeare had plenty of time to ensure that *Richard III* was as far refined as his dramatic and poetic skills then allowed, for the London theatres were closed on account of plague between June 1592 and late 1593, with only a brief opening for five weeks in January 1593. During this period, it seems, Shakespeare also wrote *Venus and Adonis*, and it has been conjectured that part, at least, of the period when the London theatres were closed was spent at Titchfield, the home of the dedicatee to that poem, the Earl of Southampton. This,

---

[1]*Greene's Groats-worth of Wit*, quoted in E.K. Chambers, *William Shakespeare* (2 vols., 1930), II, p.188.

Note:

Quotations from and references to *Richard III* are based on John Dover Wilson's edition in The New Shakespeare Series (1965). Other Shakespeare plays are cited from editions in the same Series.

however, is perhaps less likely than the view, equally a conjecture, that Shakespeare spent a good portion of this time touring the provinces with his company, the Earl of Pembroke's Servants, who were eking out a bare living by this means, and in fact are recorded as returning to London bankrupt from one such tour in August 1593.

Much surrounding the writing of *Richard III* is, then, conjecture. The date of its first performance is little less so. Philip Henslowe, the theatrical entrepreneur, records in his Diary a performance of 'Buckingam' on 30 December 1593, and three further performances (1, 10, and 27 January) within the month. These performances, which were by the Earl of Sussex's Men, probably took place at the Rose Theatre, on Bankside. Even if we accept that Henslowe's 'Buckingam' is Shakespeare's *Richard III*, however (and this is possible, given Henslowe's cavalier way with titles), there is no certainty that the 30 December performance was the first. Henslowe generally (though by no means always) marked new plays 'ne'. 'Buckingam' is not so marked, though 'Titus & Ondronicous' is on 23 January. All in all, it seems safest to assume that *Richard III* was first performed sometime prior to 30 December 1593, and that the four entries noted by Henslowe mark frequent repeats of a popular and lucrative play.

How successful *Richard III* was must be measured not in terms of the frequency of performance or the size of the takings, for in neither case do we have sufficient information even to begin such a survey, but by less direct means. One such is the frequency with which the play is alluded to in the literature of the period, another the number of editions of the play which appeared prior to the Folio of 1623. In each case *Richard III* stands very high on the list. For not only are there more contemporary allusions to it, or imitations of it, than of any other Shakespearean play except *Hamlet*, but it was produced in a number of quartos, six, equalled only by *1 Henry IV*.[2]

The reason for *Richard III*'s success is not hard to find. Like *Hamlet* and *1 Henry IV* (and indeed like contemporary non-Shakespearean successes

[2]The Quartos appeared in 1597, 1598, 1602, 1603, 1604, 1605, 1612, and 1622.

like Kyd's *Spanish Tragedy* and Marlowe's *Tamburlaine, Dr Faustus*, and *The Jew of Malta*), the play contains a central figure of immense and compelling magnetism. Richard Crookback, Duke of Gloucester and afterwards King Richard III, is what R.G. Moulton described as 'a picture of ideal villainy',[3] a figure fascinating alike in the totality of his commitment to evil and in the nonchalant ease with which he achieves his wicked ends. As such he has always been a vehicle for the greatest actors of the age. Richard Burbage, the first great virtuoso of the English stage, may well have been the original Richard Crookback, and certainly made the rôle his own, while since then Garrick, Kemble, Kean, Irving, Wolfit, and Olivier have all performed noteably in the title part, with the last translating the play, albeit conflated with parts of *3 Henry VI*, into a memorable film. After nearly four centuries, Shakespeare's first great stage creation still enjoys a steady success. In discussing and evaluating *Richard III* this study will be seeking, amongst other things, to explain why.

[3]*Shakespeare as a Dramatic Artist* (2nd ed., 1888), p.90.

2. Background

The fascinating villain who dominates *Richard III* has little to do, save in the most general sense, with the historical Richard III (1483 – 85). Even though not all historians would go so far in sympathetic revaluation of the last of the Yorkist kings as does the author of the standard modern biography, Paul Murray Kendall, and none would subscribe to the starry-eyed whitewashing which is enshrined in the Fellowship of the White Boar (in England) and the Friends of Richard III, Inc. (in the United States), it is generally agreed that Richard III was very far from the monster of vice that he is made out to be in Shakespeare's play. As E.F. Jacob most temperately puts it, 'That there was a sound constructive side to Richard III is undoubted. He was very far from being the distorted villain of tradition.'[4]

Space does not permit an account of the historical Richard's career, for which readers are referred to Kendall's *Richard III* (1955). By way of setting Shakespeare's villain in perspective, however, it may be noted that though the historical Richard was either directly guilty of, or morally responsible for, the deaths of the two 'Princes in the Tower', and certainly rid himself over-expeditiously of Lord Hastings, he had warrant for the despatch of the Woodvilles and Buckingham, who were in league against him, and was not guilty of Clarence's death (which he opposed) or that of Edward, Henry VI's son, at the Battle of Tewkesbury. Equally, though as Constable of England Richard perhaps oversaw the death of Henry VI in the Tower in 1471, it was an action carried out on the orders of Edward IV and his council, and hence not his personal responsibility.

And his deformity? His crookback? This too is myth, along with the two-year period of gestation and all the other accoutrements of monstrosity. As Paul Murray Kendall remarks:

[4] *The Fifteenth Century*, Oxford History of England (1961), VI, p.645.

Though one of Richard's shoulders was slightly higher than the other, he had no withered arm nor hunched back nor game leg; he was a prince of sensitive, even intellectual mien, probably somewhat stiff and reserved; he showed himself hardy in the exercise of arms and a successful commander; he spent his happiest years when dwelling in Yorkshire as Lord of the North, and remained popular there; as King, he proved himself, though harried, an accomplished and conscientious ruler; but he could not live down—probably in his own mind as well as in the minds of his subjects—the ruthless and violent means by which he thrust himself into power.[5]

How then did a man become a monster, the historical Richard III become the villainous hero of Shakespeare's play, a 'lump of foul deformity' and 'hell's black intelligencer'? How could the basic facts become so distorted that in *3 Henry VI* we find Richard, Duke of Gloucester, taking a ferocious part in battles fought when he was not yet nine, and espousing the *realpolitik* of Machiavelli when, in 1464, he was but 12? In answering these questions we need not merely to look at the source material of which Shakespeare made use, but also to consider what, in the sixteenth century, history was thought to be.

SHAKESPEARE'S HISTORICAL SOURCES

Geoffrey Bullough lists 15 major historical sources for the life of Richard III known to scholars in the sixteenth century, and concludes that Shakespeare knew at least five: Edward Hall's *Union of the Noble and Illustre Famelies of Lancastre and York* (1548), Richard Grafton's *Continuation of Hardying's Chronicle* (1543), Raphael Holinshed's *The Chronicles of England, Scotland and Ireland*, 2 vols. (1578), enlarged into 3 vols. (1587), Robert Fabyan's *Chronicle* (1516 et seq.), and John Stow's *Annales* (1580, 1592).[6] It seems quite possible, however, as Bullough's careful comparison of the sources and the play shows, that in fact Shakespeare used only Hall and Holinshed, since details derivable from Grafton, Fabyan, and Stow were available also in these two great chronicle sources.

[5]*Richard III: The Great Debate*, (New York, 1965), p.20.
[6]*Narrative and Dramatic Sources of Shakespeare* (6 vols., 1957–75), III, p.227.

Yet even if Shakespeare's historical reading about Richard III was limited to two works, this is not to say that no other historical writing *influenced* the composition of *Richard III*. For just as Holinshed used Hall freely in the compilation of his *Chronicles*, so Hall in turn used Grafton, and Grafton, More and Polydore Vergil. Given this complicated pattern of borrowing it is perhaps best to preface an examination of Hall and Holinshed, Shakespeare's sources proper, with a brief account of the two seminal works in the historiography of Richard III, Polydore Vergil's *Anglica Historia* and Sir Thomas More's *History of King Richard the Third*, looking there for the genesis of the monster-king whom Shakespeare so masterfully brings to completion.

VERGIL AND MORE: THE ORIGINS OF THE RICHARD MYTH

A scholar of international repute, Polydore Vergil came to England in 1502 on Papal business, and was encouraged by Henry VII to stay and to write a history of England.[7] A scholarly and sophisticated work in the new humanist manner, attentive to sources and critical of the legendary, Vergil's *Anglica Historia* (1534) has often been presented as essentially a propagandist work on behalf of the Tudors. Recent studies of Vergil discount this and its concomitant – that the history sets out deliberately to blacken Richard III's character. Certainly the portrait of the usurper-king is a black one, but as Duke of Gloucester Richard is shown in a generally favourable light, with only two crimes against him – the deaths of Henry VI (in the Tower) and of his son Prince Edward (at the Battle of Tewkesbury). That he was responsible for Clarence's death is nowhere suggested.

With Sir Thomas More's *History of King Richard III* we are at once in a different world. Here we have no loyal younger brother, as in Vergil, but one who from the first displayed characteristics which we might, anachronistically, call Machiavellian. Moreover this innate viciousness is matched, in More's portrait, by physical deformities of the type familiar to us in Shakespeare's Richard. He was, we are told, 'little of stature,

[7]On Vergil, see Alison Hanham, *Richard III and His Early Historians* (1975) pp.125 – 47.

ill-featured of limbs, crook-backed, his left shoulder much higher than his right, hard-favoured of visage and such as is in princes called warlike, in other men otherwise'.[8] As More's portrait of Richard begins, so it continues, with crime after crime attributed to him, including complicity ('some wise men also think', says More) in the murder of Clarence, and an ambition, deeply-settled well before Edward IV's death, to be king.

Inevitably, so black and vivid a portrait of Richard has led to controversy, with historians taking sides for or against More just as (and indeed largely according to the way) they take sides for or against Richard. Current thinking, however, tends to see the *History* less as history than as literature, and to stress the work's dramatic qualities rather than fidelity to fact, so much so that the most recent investigator of Richard III's reputation can argue that the *History* forms 'in some important respects ... a lucianic, and so irreverent, comment on the whole craft of history', and that 'it is more profitable to regard it as literature than as a work of scholarship embodying the results of historical research'.[9]

Whatever modern historiographers may think, however, More was certainly taken during the sixteenth century to be as fully in possession of the facts as Polydore Vergil, while the strongly dramatic narrative, with its many reputedly verbatim conversations between the principal characters, naturally attracted far wider attention than did Vergil's sober Latin account. Hence it is More who, despite the fact that his *History* is unfinished, chiefly moulds the thinking of Tudor historians, and indirectly, therefore, provides the basis for Shakespeare's magnificent villain.

HALL AND HOLINSHED: THE MYTH DEVELOPED

More's *History* was written in 1513, but not published until 1557. Like Vergil's *Historia*, however, it was well known in manuscript, and Hall made extensive use of it in the 1540s, employing Vergil only where More

---

[8] I quote from the text of More's *History* given in Kendall's *Great Debate*, p.35.
[9] Hanham, p.155.

was not available. A reading of *The Union of the Noble and Illustre Fameles of Lancastre and Yorke* (1548) reveals why. Hall is clearly interested in the dramatic representation of history, and he seizes on such elements in More, developing and amplifying them both by borrowing from Vergil and by the creation of additional dialogue. Even in making the usurping Richard III a tyrant and murderer of the blackest kind, however, he does not entirely abandon the facts as transmitted by Vergil. For having remarked on the young Richard's fidelity to his brother and skill in war, Hall concludes that if he had not aspired beyond the Protectorship, 'no doubt but the realme had prospered, and he much praysed and beloved as he is nowe abhorred and vilipended'.[10]

Hall not only builds up the dramatic effect by developing the black Richard transmitted to him by More, but also by contrasting the usurper's villainy with the innocence of his young victims – the two Princes in the Tower are now 'innocent babes' – and the transcendant virtue of his opponent. In Hall, the Earl of Richmond is presented as 'so formed and decorated with all gyftes and lyniamentes of nature that he semed more an angelical creature then a terrestiall personage', while his speech to his troops at Bosworth – invented (as is Richard's to *his* troops) by Hall – is delivered 'with such gesture of his body and smiling countenaunce, as though all redye he had vanquyshed hys enemies and gotten the spoyle'.

This heightening of the portrait of Richmond, effective as it is, serves not only immediate ends, however, but also wider dramatic and thematic purposes. The title Hall gave his work points to his grand design in writing the history, while the remainder of the title page develops it more fully in describing how the 'continuall dissension of the crown of this noble realm . . . beginning at the time of King Henry the Fourth, the first author of this division' is solved by the marriage of Henry VII and Elizabeth of York, and crowned by the 'reign of the high and provident prince, King Henry the Eighth, the indubitable flower and very heir of the said lineages'. The whole work is designed to develop and

---

[10]Hall's *Union* is cited in the selections provided by Bullough in *Narrative and Dramatic Sources of Shakespeare* III, pp.249 – 301.

illustrate this theme, and to do it dramatically. Even the chapter headings emphasize this:

   i The unquiet time of King Henry the Fourth.
   ii The victorious acts of King Henry the Fifth.
  iii The troublous season of King Henry the Sixth.
  iv The prosperous reign of King Edward the Fourth.
   v The pitiful life of King Edward the Fifth.
  vi The tragical doings of King Richard the Third.
 vii The politic governance of King Henry the Seventh.
viii The triumphant reign of King Henry the Eighth.

Commenting on these headings, E.M.W. Tillyard remarks:

> Hall knew and rejoiced that this list can provide more than one pattern. There were four successful and four unsuccessful kings in his list and they fall into a sort of drama form. Call the unsuccessful *a* and the successful *b*, and you get the form *a b a b a a b b*. It was not for nothing, too, that the *victorious acts* of Henry V are matched by the *tragical doings* of Richard III. *Acts* or *doings* are confined to these two kings, whose history is presented in a quite exceptionally dramatic manner.[11]

With Hall the mythic Richard III is nearly completed, with amplifications and inventions adding to the formidable portrait to which Shakespeare was heir. It is Hall who devises an account of Prince Edward's capture and death at Tewkesbury, for instance, who explains Burdet's case, referred to by Buckingham (III, v, 75 – 8), adds the taunting response of Richard to Buckingham's request for the Earldom of Hereford, Buckingham's abhorrence of the murder of the princes, the flood which destroys Buckingham's army and the couplet found on Norfolk's gate (or, in the play, on his tent, V,iii, 304 – 5). Raphael Holinshed takes over all this material and to it adds very little, save a visit to Exeter, in which Richard is dismayed at the Rougemont – Richmond resemblance (IV, ii, 100 – 4), and the bleeding of Henry VI's wounds (I, ii, 55 – 9).

[11]*Shakespeare's History Plays* (1962), p.43.

Nonetheless, Holinshed's account of Richard emerges as, if anything, blacker even than Hall's, not least because it is a truncated version of the earlier work. *The Chronicles of England, Scotland and Ireland* (2 vols. 1578, enlarged to 3 vols. 1587) is enormous in scope, extending as it does from Noah to Queen Elizabeth. Hall's *Union*, by contrast, covers a century and a half of solely English history. In abbreviating Hall, Holinshed not only condenses and paraphrases but, in the case of Richard, omits references to his earlier and better qualities. It is the last stage in the progression from the recognizably historical Richard III (in Vergil) to the mythic monster-king, child-murderer, and usurper.

SHAKESPEARE'S LITERARY SOURCES

The major historical sources for *Richard III* are, as has been said, Hall's *Union* and Holinshed's *Chronicles*. From these two works Shakespeare could derive both a fully developed myth involving a monster-king and an overall moral design involving the suffering and redemption of England.

So egregiously interesting a reign as Richard's did not only capture Shakespeare's interest, however, and there are several literary works written prior to *Richard III* which can claim in some degree to be sources for his play. One is the anonymous *True Tragedy of Richard III*. Published in 1594, but almost certainly written in 1590 or '91, the *True Tragedy* seems to have been in many respects a crude play, though its merits are difficult to assess in the only surviving text, a 'bad' or reported Quarto. Nonetheless there are a number of striking verbal parallels between it and *Richard III*, including one involving the most famous line in the latter, 'A horse! a horse! my kingdom for a horse!' (V,iv, 7).[12] There is also a parallel in structure, for as in *Richard III* so in the *True Tragedy* the material is organized around a single dominating figure. Moreover the two plays adopt a similar approach to problems of organization, unifying the episodic material by compressing and in some cases altering the chronological sequence.

[12]See Bullough, p.238.

Besides the *True Tragedy* there is one other direct literary source, namely *The Mirror for Magistrates*. First published in 1559, this collection of moral tales along the lines of Boccaccio's *De Casibus Virorum Illustrorum* and its English translation, Lydgate's *Fall of Princes*, set out to show, through 'examples passed in this realme', 'With howe greueous plagues, vyces are punished in great princes and magistrates, and how frayle and vnstable worldly prosperity is founde, where fortune seemeth moste highly to fauour.'[13] The 1559 edition of *The Mirror* contained three tales relevant to the period covered by *Richard III*: Baldwin's *Henry VI* and *George, Duke of Clarence*; and Skelton's *Edward IV*. The 1563 edition added six more, including Baldwin's *Sir Anthony Woodvile, Lord Rivers*, and Seager's *Richard Plantagenet, Duke of Gloucester*. These nine tales, which chiefly follow Hall in their material, vary greatly in quality, and it is no surprise to find that Shakespeare ignores most of them, including the very badly written *Richard Plantagenet*. He may, as Bullough notes (p.233), have taken Rivers' dream from Baldwin's *Rivers* as the germ of Clarence's dream (I,iv, 9 – 63), though the latter is more akin, in substance, to Sackville's visionary journey to Hell in the Induction, but the only certain borrowings are from Baldwin's *Clarence*. The latter's 'And in a butte of Malmesey standing by,/ Newe Christned me, because I should not crie' (370 – 1) is clearly alluded to, for instance, in Richard's punning 'Belike his majesty hath some intent/ That you should be new-christ'ned in the Tower' (I,i, 49 – 50), while the section in Baldwin dealing with the 'G' prophecy (lines 180 – 9) seems to be the basis of Richard's

> This day should Clarence closely be mewed up,
> About a prophecy, which says that G
> Of Edward's heirs the murderer shall be. (I,i, 38 – 40)

It is also worth noting that *The Mirror* was the first work to state unequivocally that Richard was directly responsible for his brother's death, and though this assertion was repeated in the *True Tragedy*, it seems not improbable, given Shakespeare's evident interest in *Clarence*,

[13]*The Mirror for Magistrates*, ed. Lily B. Campbell (New York, 1960), p.517. The text of *Clarence* is cited from this edition.

that this tale provided that facet of Shakespeare's villain also.

RICHARD III *AND THE FIRST TETRALOGY*

Shakespeare wrote 10 plays with English history as their subject. Two stand apart: *King John* and *Henry VIII*. The other eight fall into two clearly defined groups of four, and are generally accepted as having been written as such. Together these tetralogies span nearly a century of English history from Richard II to Henry VII in terms very similar to Edward Hall's *Union of Lancastre and Yorke*, linking the beginning of civil strife with the deposition of a rightful king and showing its end in the death of a usurper and the accession of a peacemaker.

Whether or not Shakespeare conceived these tetralogies jointly, need not, fortunately, be debated here. What is of concern is the nature and significance of the links between *Richard III* and the three parts of *Henry VI* which with it form the first tetralogy. Tillyard takes the tetralogic case to its furthest point when he argues that 'the main business of the play is to complete the national tetralogy and to display the working out of God's plan to restore England to prosperity'.[14] The weakness of this argument lies in the assumption that the completion of the tetralogy entails the subordination of Richard to an overall design. The analysis of the play which is to follow will seek to show that the completion of the tetralogy and the creation of the dominating villain-hero are complementary rather than exclusive. It will argue, to put it another way, that Hall's moral history and More's lucianic portrait of a tyrant are both contained in *Richard III*.

Tillyard's view of the primacy of the tetralogy over the individual play leads him to argue further that 'in its function of summing up and completing what has gone before, *Richard III* inevitably suffers as a detached unit', and to conclude that 'it is a confused affair without the memory of Clarence's perjury to Warwick before Coventry, of Queen Margaret's crowning of York with a paper crown before stabbing him at Wakefield, and of the triple murder of Prince Edward at Tewkesbury'.[15]

---

[14]*Shakespeare's History Plays*, p.199.
[15]*Ibid.*, p.199.

Again the case seems overstated. It is true that there are many points in *Richard III* where a precise knowledge of what has gone before may enhance our understanding and enjoyment. Yet nowhere in the play is it essential. Even amidst the easily confusing lists of Edwards and Richards the overall point is clear: an apt retribution is taking place. Knowledge of the three parts of *Henry VI* will at times particularize that sense of aptness, but not in any sense modify it.

This duality in *Richard III* — a separate entity which is also the culmination of a tetralogy — is clearly observable in the first two acts of the play, where Shakespeare's drastic manipulation of chronology, which makes the death of Henry VI (1471), the wooing of Anne (1472), the imprisonment and death of Clarence (1477 – 8), and the death of Edward IV (1483) more or less contemporaneous, serves both to link the new play to its predecessor chronologically, eliminating what would otherwise be a break in time and causality, and to give the new action — and the new central figure — a massive initial impetus. Richard's opening soliloquy is equally dual-purpose, for where on the one hand it makes a magnificently comprehensive and dramatic initiation into his villainy, on the other it is no initiation at all, but rather a renewal of his commitment to evil made first in soliloquy following Edward IV's wooing of Lady Grey (*3 Henry VI* III,ii, 124 – 95), and reiterated after the stabbing of Henry VI (V, vi, 68 – 93).

The final act of *Richard III* also has a double purpose. In Richmond's victory speech, for instance, we find an unmistakable expression of the larger theme so insistently promulgated by Hall – the union in marriage of the divided houses of Lancaster and York (V,v, 27 – 31). Yet in the same speech we also find ironic echoes of the opening soliloquy (Richmond's 'smooth-faced peace' taking up Richard's 'Grim-visag'd war hath smoothed his wrinkled front'), while elsewhere in the final act similar recollective (and ironic) references occur. Richard, for instance, makes much before Bosworth of the refusal of the sun to shine (V,iii, 277 – 82). This not only contrasts with Richmond's earlier – and more cheerful – remarks upon the setting sun (V,iii, 19 – 21), but harks back with it to the opening lines of Richard's first soliloquy, with its punning reference to the sun as the emblem of the House of York:

Now is the winter of our discontent
Made glorious summer by this sun of York;
And all the clouds that loured upon our house
In the deep bosom of the ocean buried. (I,i, 1 – 4)

By such means as these, and others which will be demonstrated as this analysis proceeds, Shakespeare underlines the artistic unity of *Richard III* as well as the coherence of the tetralogy of which it forms a part.

3. The Play

Richard III is a highly formal play. Its stylized speeches, its overtly patterned scenes and its obviously symbolic tableaux are immediately evident, and a closer reading only serves to increase the sense of the formal and the patterned in speech and action. With so early a play the obvious temptation is to attribute this to Shakespeare's inexperience. This explanation is invalidated, however, by a comparison with the three Shakespeare plays which undoubtedly precede *Richard III*. For though all three parts of *Henry VI* are at times as strongly patterned and formal as *Richard III*, not one of them approaches the last part of the tetralogy in the consistency of this patterning. *Richard III* is, indeed, unique in the Shakespeare canon in that consistency, and the inescapable conclusion to be drawn from this and from the carefully overt nature of so much of the stylization is that it constitutes a choice on Shakespeare's part. What follows is designed not only to show the nature and extent of these formal elements but also to suggest why Shakespeare chose to rely so heavily upon them.

FORMALITY: THE LANGUAGE

That the language of *Richard III* is to a high degree formal may not be so apparent to a twentieth-century audience as it would have been to one of the sixteenth, but even to an age uninstructed in the arts of rhetoric there is clearly something special, linguistically, about a passage such as this:

> *Anne*   I would I knew thy heart.
> *Gloucester*   'Tis figured in my tongue.
> *Anne*   I fear me both are false.
> *Gloucester*   Then never was man true.
> *Anne*   Well, well, put up your sword.
> *Gloucester*   Say, then, my peace is made.

Anne   That shalt thou know hereafter.
Gloucester   But shall I live in hope?
Anne   All men, I hope, live so.
Gloucester   Vouchsafe to wear this ring.
Anne   To take is not to give.   [*she puts on the ring*]

(I, ii, 192 – 201)

An Elizabethan to any degree educated would be ready enough to name the rhetorical device employed here as stichomythia, and to describe the finer points of this antithetical exchange, or that more complex example which occurs earlier in the same scene (I, ii, 68 – 84).

Even without the technical vocabulary with which Shakespeare's contemporaries were equipped, however, we can determine the nature of these passages and describe their dramatic effects. Richard himself refers at line 115 to 'this keen encounter of our wits', and clearly these two passages are very like the witty skirmishes in which lovers indulge in *Love's Labours Lost*, or *Much Ado About Nothing*. In the circumstances, this is highly ironic, since Anne is here expressing not her attraction towards Richard but her loathing of him. Yet the irony is a double one since this 'keen encounter' actually ends in a successful wooing, as Anne is won over by the brilliant effrontery of Richard. The very use of this antithetical form of dialogue, therefore, is itself of advantage to Shakespeare.

There are other advantages, too, to be derived from such overtly stylized exchanges as these. I,ii opens with Anne mourning her murdered father-in-law Henry VI, and confronting in Richard his murderer and her husband's. It ends with their betrothal. Even allowing for the conventional Elizabethan view of woman's changeability and for the dramatic convention of instantaneous conversion, this strains credibility – or would, if the strains of credibility were put upon the scene. That they are not is due in large part to the succession of devices, mainly linguistic, which like stychomythia, distance the audience from the characters and prevent identification. Anne's opening speech, for instance, is cast very clearly in the form of a lament, and as such follows established conventions in language and structure. There is a highly rhetorical opening, for instance, with a parenthetical second line picking up in ironic terms the key phrase from the first and leading to the announcement of the lament and to a series of formal elegiac phrases:

Anne Set down, set down, set down your honourable load –
If honour may be shrouded in a hearse –
Whilst I awhile obsequiously lament
Th 'untimely fall of virtuous Lancaster. (I,ii, 1 – 4)

This is followed by a traditional invocation involving also an equally traditional self-description on the part of the speaker (5 – 11), and this, in its turn, by a formal imprecation, a curse solemnly delivered against the cause of the grief (14 – 20). The lament ends, as formally as it began, with the recapitulatory 'Rest you, whiles I lament King Henry's corse' (32). It is followed by the entry of Richard and two stylized speeches from Anne, one involving the highly ritual 'Avaunt, thou dreadful minister of hell!' (46) and the other a solemn call for vengeance (62 – 7). These, in their turn, are followed by the first of the 'exchanges of wit' to which reference was made earlier. Finally, with Anne won despite the odds, Richard exults in a soliloquy which opens with 'Was ever woman in this humour wooed?/ Was ever woman in this humour won?' (I,ii, 227 – 8), and ends with an ironic self-reappraisal which is clearly meant to be read with his opening soliloquy in mind (compare I,ii, 252 – 63 and I,i, 14 – 27).

Not every line in I,ii is formal and rhetorical. Indeed there are lines, like that in Richard's final soliloquy, 'I'll have her; but I will not keep her long' (229), which by their colloquial tone contrast strongly with the remainder. In general, however, I,ii is linguistically formal. As such it is characteristic of the play as a whole. Formality is the norm.

Why is this so? For what I take to be the primary reason we should, perhaps, look at one of the most formal and rhetorical scenes of all, IV,iv. It opens with a speech from Queen Margaret, who in defiance of all the historical or quasi-historical accounts, has 'slily . . . lurked' on the edge of the action since I,iii. Though cast as a soliloquy, the speech is essentially a prologue, and cast in terms which emphasize this function:

So now prosperity begins to mellow
And drop into the rotten mouth of death.

Here in these confines slily have I lurked,
To watch the waning of mine enemies.
A dire induction am I witness to,
And will to France, hoping the consequence
Will prove as bitter, black, and tragical. (IV,iv, 1 – 7)

Margaret sees herself as a 'witness', set 'to watch', and lines 1, 2, and 4
(where 'waning' implies a previous 'waxing') make it clear that she
expects to observe the further turning of Fortune's wheel.

The entry of Queen Elizabeth and the old Duchess of York brings the
scene proper, with a lament formally announced by Queen Elizabeth in
her apostrophe to her dead sons (9–14), and taken up by the Duchess,
with Margaret adding telling asides. At line 35, goaded by Queen
Elizabeth's 'Ah, who hath any cause to mourn but we?', she joins them
and catalogues her losses and theirs:

I had an Edward, till a Richard killed him;
I had a Harry, till a Richard killed him:
Thou hadst an Edward, till a Richard killed him;
Thou hadst a Richard, till a Richard killed him. (40 – 3)

Joined in this confusing catalogue by the Duchess, Margaret first gives
thanks to God for the 'hell-hound' Richard, and then resumes the
cataloguing, enlarging the scope to include those outside the royal
families of Lancaster and York,

The beholders of this frantic play,
Th'adulterate Hastings, Rivers, Vaughan, Grey,
Untimely smothered in their dusky graves. (68 – 70)

In referring to Hastings, Rivers, and the rest as 'beholders' caught up
in this 'frantic play', Margaret suggests that what has occurred has been
akin to a play within a play, a dramatic action now enlarging to include
those who were formerly only spectators. The metaphor is strengthened
by recollection of two phrases in Margaret's opening soliloquy, the
prologue-like speech in which she spoke of herself as a 'witness' to 'a dire
induction' which would, she hoped, prove 'black, and tragical'. The
terms may, of course, have their origin in *The Mirror for Magistrates*, one

of Shakespeare's certain sources, but they are also dramatic, and as such they serve to reinforce the idea of the 'frantic play' and prepare us for the more extended statement which follows:

> I called thee then vain flourish of my fortune;
> I called thee then poor shadow, painted queen,
> The presentation of but what I was;
> The flattering index of a direful pageant;
> One heaved a-high, to be hurled down below;
> A mother only mocked with two fair babes;
> A dream of what thou wast, a garish flag,
> To be the aim of every dangerous shot;
> A sign of dignity, a breath, a bubble;
> A queen in jest, only to fill the scene. (IV, iv, 82 – 91)

As later in *Henry V*, so here Shakespeare seems intent on heightening our sense of the play *as a play*. In *Henry V* the chorus fulfils this function, providing a device for presenting episodic material in a set of epic tableaux which reveal to us successive facets of the ideal king. In *Richard III* the stress is rather different. The point here is the steady forward movement of history; the inexorable on-turning of fortune's wheel, whereby 'one [is] heaved a-high, to be hurled down below', and those participating in the 'direful pageant' are by 'the course of Justice whirled about', and left 'a very prey to time' (105 – 6). Carefully placed at half a remove from the action, Queen Margaret is endowed with a choric voice by turns prophetic, admonitory, and recapitulatory. Here, though, she serves to reveal, through her own perception of the action to which she is an adjunct, the organizing principle for the entire play and the ultimate explanation for the sustained rhetoric of the language. Distancing us by its formality and consciously structured nature, the language serves to reinforce the sense of an action which is acknowledged even by its partici- pants to be 'dramatic'.

The remainder of IV,iv serves well to illustrate the contribution of language to this pageant effect. The Duchess of York asks 'Why should calamity be full of words?' (126). Queen Elizabeth's answer is the con- ventional wisdom of words easing feelings, but Shakespeare's is clearly more complex. For both the question, with its careful underlining of the rhetorical, and the rhetoric itself serve the wider purposes of the pageant. Queen Margaret, who formerly supplied the choric lamentation, is gone, and the Duchess and Queen Elizabeth take up both her rôle and, to some extent, her style. Margaret, for instance, had devoted part of her great lament to the traditional *topos* of 'Ubi Sunt',

> Where is thy husband now? where be thy brothers?
> Where be thy two sons? wherein dost thou joy? (IV,iv, 92 – 3)

a theme which the Duchess and Queen Elizabeth take up also (145 – 8). Equally, the Duchess takes over the task of cursing, previously Margaret's, adding to it the particular intensity and significance of a mother's curse (IV,iv, 184–96) – a curse which is clearly meant to remind us of the earlier blessing, so blasphemously mocked by Richard (II,ii, 107–10).

Linked to the 'Ubi Sunt' *topos* in Margaret's 'pageant' speech is a second traditional lamentation theme, 'Then and Now'. Margaret developed it powerfully in relation to both the concepts of fortune's wheel and the pageant (82–91 and 97–113). In the remainder of the scene we experience this relationship between past and present in language and in action. The Duchess's curse, as has been remarked, contrasts with her earlier blessing. So, equally but on a far larger scale, the wooing, through her mother, of Princess Elizabeth recalls the earlier wooing of Anne. Equally as stylized linguistically, and essentially alike in situation, with Richard striving to succeed in the least propitious of circumstances, the second wooing distances us in the same fashion as the first, but more powerfully, since it adds to the earlier experience the sense of the cyclic, the repeated, the consciously patterned event.

FORMALITY: THE ACTION

The pervasive formality in language, which is so crucial a feature of *Richard III*, is matched, as might be expected, by an equally pervasive formality in the action. What this patterning means to the play as a whole will be considered first in a significant example at the level of the microcosmic, then by an examination of the larger structures which reveal the same approach and which, in turn, point to the overall design of the play. It will also be shown how close the links are between the patterning of the language and the patterning of the action.

CHARACTER ENTRY AND INTRODUCTION

One of the easiest targets for the unsympathetic critic intent on exposing the immaturity of Shakespeare's dramaturgy in *Richard III* would be his general method of introducing his characters. In I,i, for instance, we find the entry of Clarence prefaced by 'Dive, thoughts, down to my soul – here Clarence comes' (41) and that of Hastings by 'But who comes here? the new-delivered Hastings?' (121). In III,v, similarly, the entry of the Mayor and Catesby is prefaced by

> *Buckingham*   But what, is Catesby gone?
> *Gloucester*   He is; and see, he brings the mayor along. (12–13)

Numerous examples of these obvious introductions could be cited, many of them involving an element of the pat, or conveniently coincidental. As with the language, however, so here in the combination of language and action, the obvious is a stratagem, the patterned intentionally overt. Once again, it seems, Shakespeare is working to stress the element of the pageant, to develop and maintain our sense of the play as a play.

In doing this, however, Shakespeare is also developing an aspect of the play not yet discussed: the special rôle of Richard. For just as the linguistic patterning of IV,iv places Queen Margaret outside the pageant, so the studied introductions help to place Richard outside it also. This is not merely due to the fact that it is he who makes the majority of these stagey statements (although by this means he is in a sense placed apart and in communication with us in the same way as in a soliloquy) but also to the fact that those introductions made by others heighten the sense which Richard's create of being part of a pattern of activity which is, if not organized, then at least exploited by him. Three times, for instance, Buckingham, Richard's principal henchman, remarks on the 'good time' in which characters arrive. In each case the timeliness furthers Richard's cause, and reinforces the sense created by the dramatic action as a whole of the effortless progression of the 'direful pageant' in the direction chosen by Richard. In this connection it is significant that these opportune 'introduced' entries cease at the moment when, in Act IV, Richard's fortunes begin to flag and Richmond's to prosper.

NEMESIS

Writ large, the same sense of an effortless progression in the pageant is found in the series of Nemesis actions which constitute almost the entire plot of *Richard III*. First described by R.G. Moulton in his classic study of the play, these Nemesis actions involve, successively, Clarence, King Edward, the Queen's kindred, Rivers, Grey, and Vaughan, Hastings, Buckingham, and the women, Lady Anne and Queen Elizabeth, while a final Nemesis action destroys the key figure in all the other retributive actions, Richard himself.

1. *Clarence*

The Nemesis action involving George, Duke of Clarence, has already begun when the play opens. Through Richard's plotting, his brother has been arrested and makes his first appearance on his way under guard to the Tower. Plunging us *in media res*, this opening is not only dramatically powerful but also an effective way of demonstrating the continuity of action which constitutes the pageant of history. Clarence, fickle and in *3 Henry VI* twice forsworn, bears at the outset a heavier burden of guilt than anyone save Richard, and hence is the first to feel the force of retribution.

In his analysis of the Nemesis actions, Moulton pointed out not only that Shakespeare repeats essentially the same pattern in each case, but also that in each he uses the same means (prophecy, irony, and recognition) of emphasizing the repetition of the pattern. Yet despite this, the dramatist does make each of the retributive actions individually appropriate. In Clarence's case, for instance, there is no advance notice in the form of prophecy, such as occurs in every other case through the utterances of Queen Margaret. What we have instead is the dream, with its intensely dramatic mingling of guilt, fear, and premonition leading to the encounter in hell between the dead Clarence and those he betrayed, Warwick and Prince Edward (I,iv, 48 – 57).

Nor is there the opportunity for the ironies of the kind prevalent in the later Nemesis actions, where a statement of supreme self-confidence by the unsuspecting victim generally precedes the stroke of retribution. In its place, however, we find bitterly ironic statements dependent on Clarence's trust in his brother Richard:

> Bid Gloucester think of this, and he will weep.
> *1 Murderer*   Ay, millstones, as he lessoned us to weep.
> *Clarence*   O, do not slander him, for he is kind.
> *1 Murderer*   As snow in harvest. Come, you deceive yourself:
> 'Tis he that sends us to destroy you here. (I,iv, 239 – 43)

While the circumstances of the Clarence plot somewhat limit the elements of prophecy and irony, however, they allow unusually full play to the third of Moulton's typical Nemesis elements – recognition. For not only does Clarence himself acknowledge his complicity in 'misdeeds' for which he expects God's vengeance, but during his pleading with the Murderers he is forced by them to recognize the aptness of the retribution he is facing, and to see that he cannot invoke divine laws when he himself has broken them:

> Take heed; for he holds vengeance in his hand,
> To hurl upon their heads that break his law.
> *2 Murderer*   And that same vengeance doth he hurl on thee,
> For false forswearing, and for murder too:
> Thou didst receive the sacrament to fight
> In quarrel of the house of Lancaster.
> *1 Murderer*   And, like a traitor to the name of God,
> Didst break that vow, and with thy treacherous blade
> Unrip'st the bowels of thy sov'reign's son.
> *2 Murderer*   Whom thou wast sworn to cherish and defend.
> *1 Murderer*   How canst thou urge God's dreadful law to us,
> When thou has broke it in such dear degree? (I,iv, 199–210)

Demolished by the merciless logic of the Murderers – in this as in so much else the true associates of Richard – Clarence's case collapses, and with it the case of every other victim of Nemesis in the play.[16] The Duke may plead for mercy, like others after him, but the protection of the law, divine or human, has been forfeited, and retribution is certain.

2. King Edward

The Clarence plot is very fully developed, thematically and artistically. That centring on King Edward, by contrast, is the briefest in the play. Yet even so, Shakespeare manages to develop a typical Nemesis pattern. The prophetic element comes as part of Queen Margaret's curse in I,iii, when she says, 'Though not by war, by surfeit die your king,/ As ours, by murder, to make him a king!' (I,iii, 197 – 8), while the irony, which lies in the fact that Richard, through the murder of Clarence, has destroyed the peace Edward is trying to build even before the process is begun, is expressed most powerfully in the opening lines of Act II:

> King Edward   Why, so: now have I done a good day's work.
> You peers, continue this united league:
> I every day expect an embassage
> From my Redeemer to redeem me hence;
> And more at peace my soul shall part to heaven,
> Since I have made my friends at peace on earth. (II,i, 1–6)

Recognition of guilt comes, in its turn, when Lord Stanley pleads so powerfully for his servant's life, and the King recognizes the contrast with his own behaviour:

> Have I a tongue to doom my brother's death,
> And shall that tongue give pardon to a slave?
> My brother killed no man – his fault was thought,
> And yet his punishment was bitter death. (II,i, 103–6)

Blaming himself for the 'brutish wrath' which led him to forget Clarence's virtues and remember only his faults, Edward devotes his last utterances to a direct acknowledgement of his guilt, and that of those around him:

[16]Except the two women, who suffer more for their involvement with their sinning menfolk than for their own sins.

O God, I fear thy justice will take hold
On me, and you, and mine, and yours, for this!
Come, Hastings, help me to my closet. Ah, poor Clarence! (II,i,
132–4)

Though, as Queen Margaret so rightly prophesied, King Edward dies of
'surfeit' rather than violently, it is clear that we are meant to see his death
as just as retributive as the others.

3. *Rivers, Grey, and Vaughan*

Somewhat unlucky, it might be thought, to have been included in Queen
Margaret's curse as by-standers when her son was murdered, Rivers and
his kinsmen, Grey and Vaughan, are light-weights, dramatically, and
hence are treated, in the third of the Nemesis actions, collectively as well
as briefly. Shakespeare takes the opportunity provided by their insignifi-
cance, however, to vary the presentation of the retributive process.
Hence we do not see the arrest of the three, but merely hear of it as part of
a discussion between Hastings and Stanley (III,ii, 82 – 5).

Given a brief death-scene, the three debate the justice of their deaths,
with Rivers proclaiming his innocence, but Grey recognizing the opera-
tion of a retributive causality:

Now Margaret's curse is fall'n upon our heads,
When she exclaimed on Hastings, you, and I,
For standing by when Richard stabbed her son. (III,iii, 14–16)

Ironically, however, it is the imperceptive Rivers who provides the most
significant statement in the scene when he remarks:

O Pomfret, Pomfret! O thou bloody prison,
Fatal and ominous to noble peers!
Within the guilty closure of thy walls
Richard the Second here was hacked to death;
And, for more slander to thy dismal seat,
We give to thee our guiltless blood to drink. (III,iii, 8–13)

Rivers himself finds only coincidence here, but Shakespeare, placing the
remark with a precision made to seem casual right at the mid-point of the

play, is clearly drawing our attention to the wider meaning of what is happening, and going beyond the limits even of the tetralogy to relate, *à la* Hall, 'the tragical doings of King Richard the Third' to the reasons for 'the unquiet time of King Henry the Fourth' and all that followed.

4. *Hastings*

Though the Nemesis actions are presented in series, with the similarity of each to each stressed by repetition, Shakespeare takes great care also to ensure that the series is not merely a succession of events, but exhibits a developing form. Hence we find the most important Nemesis actions placed first and last, with the remainder set out in ascending order of importance between the two. With Hastings, we reach the third of the five intervening retributive patterns, and it is at once clear that though the elements remain the same, the action is to be developed on a larger scale and more intricately than was the case with King Edward or Rivers, Grey, and Vaughan.

We first encounter Hastings in I,i, following his release from the Tower. His response to Richard's enquiry, 'How hath your lordship brooked imprisonment?', is a characteristic combination of self-confidence and retributive zeal (125 – 8), further demonstrated in III,ii, where the ironic component in the Nemesis action is developed ever more strongly as he first rejects the warning brought by Stanley's herald (19–33), then talks successively to Catesby, Stanley, a Pursuivant, a Priest, and Buckingham. The dominant tone is established in the conversation with Catesby (60 – 8), reinforced in the exchange with Stanley, whose caution contrasts so strongly with Hastings' 'Think you, but that I know our state secure, / I would be so triumphant as I am?' (80–1), and brought to a high point in the quite unnecessary chat with the Pursuivant:

How now, sirrah? how goes the world with thee?
Pursuivant   The better that your lordship please to ask.
Hastings   I tell thee, man, 'tis better with me now
Than when thou met'st me last where now we meet:
Then was I going prisoner to the Tower,

By the suggestion of the queen's allies;
By now, I tell thee (keep it to thyself)
This day those enemies are put to death,
And I in better state than e'er I was. (III,ii, 95–103)

In *Richard III*, of course, such *hubris* as this can only precede a fall. In Hastings' case this ensues with brutal suddenness, beautifully engineered by Buckingham and Richard, and leaving the victim nothing to do but lament his folly and his guilt:

O, now I need the priest that spake to me:
I now repent I told the pursuivant,
As too triumphing, how mine enemies
To-day at Pomfret bloodily were butchered,
And I myself secure in grace and favour.
O Margaret, Margaret, now thy heavy curse
Is lighted on poor Hastings' wretched head! (III,iv, 86–92)

5. *Buckingham*

When in I,iii Queen Margaret utters the curse which leaves Hastings' hair standing on end (304), she does not extend it to Buckingham, but on the contrary offers to kiss his hand 'in sign of league and amity' (282), and tries to warn him of the dangers involved in associating with Richard. This incident distinguishes Buckingham from the other victims of Nemesis. Unlike them, he has played no part in the murderous feuding of *Henry VI* and hence begins the play with no inheritance of guilt. That he, too, becomes a victim of the retributive process is due entirely to his own actions and choices, which make him a willing tool for Richard's use.

And here again is a feature which sets Buckingham apart from the rest. Like them he eventually suffers at Richard's hands, but unlike them he first becomes Richard's collaborator and aide, actively engaged in bringing the latter's villainy to fruition and in destroying his opponents. By III,i he is firmly established as Richard's right-hand man, and the ensuing scenes show the bonds grow steadily stronger. It is he, for instance, who persuades the Cardinal to entice the young Duke of York from sanctuary, and he who tutors Catesby on how to sound out Hastings concerning the usurpation. Equally it is he who helps Richard destroy Hastings in III,iv, and who in III,v and III,vii stage-manages Richard's 'reluctant' acceptance of the crown.

It is in these scenes, III,v and vii, that Buckingham reaches the high point of his career. Like Richard, he enjoys nothing more than playing a part, whether it be simulating fear while dressed 'in rotten armour, marvellous ill-favoured', as the stage-direction has it, persuading the reluctant citizenry of Richard's right to the throne or, most enjoyably of all, urging a pious and other-worldly Lord Protector that it is his duty to assume the cares and burdens of monarchy. Nor is it only the acting that Buckingham enjoys. For such dissimulation as this brings with it a host of ironies, and the Duke, 'the deep-revolving witty Buckingham', as Richard calls him, revels in these also. And here again there is a clear difference between Buckingham and the earlier victims of Nemesis. For where each of them is touched by irony, it is as the unconscious object of it. With Buckingham, as with Richard, however, the irony is consciously felt to be working for the perpetrator.

In so tightly structured a scheme of things, of course, such a situation cannot last long. And Buckingham's downfall comes, predictably, immediately following his greatest triumph. Questioned by the newly crowned Richard as to his attitude to the killing of the princes in the Tower, he prevaricates and then, pressed, asks for time to consider. In this moment he is lost. Like Hastings, he has long acquiesced in Richard's schemes, and like Hastings, he is ruthlessly cast aside at the first moment's hesitancy. The irony is that in each case the cause is a moral objection. Hastings refuses to countenance the deposition of Edward V and is immediately marked for destruction. Buckingham, likewise, hesitates over the killing of the princes, and is marked also.

Having made one mistake, Buckingham immediately compounds it with another as disastrous in pressing the angry and distracted Richard for the Earldom of Hereford, before realizing his danger and fleeing to Wales. There, historically, he posed a considerable threat to Richard, but in the play he becomes a dramatic nonentity, occasionally mentioned but never taken seriously save (ironically) at the moment when his army is 'dispersed and scattered;/ And he himself wand'red away alone' (IV,iv, 512–13). Only in his death-scene, the most significant since Clarence's, does Buckingham regain his importance with a speech of recognition and contrition which in its explicitness serves not only to sum up his own plight but also, representatively, that of every other victim of Nemesis:

> This is All-Souls' day, fellow, is it not?
> *Sheriff*   It is, my lord.
> *Buckingham*   Why, then All-Souls' day is my body's doomsday.
> This is the day which in King Edward's time
> I wished might fall on me when I was found
> False to his children and his wife's allies;
> This is the day wherein I wished to fall
> By the false faith of him whom most I trusted;
> This, this All-Souls' day to my fearful soul
> Is the determined respite of my wrongs:
> That high All-Seer which I dallied with
> Hath turned my feigned prayer on my head,
> And given in earnest what I begged in jest.
> Thus doth He force the swords of wicked men
> To turn their own points in their masters' bosoms:
> Thus Margaret's curse falls heavy on my neck;
> 'When he,' quoth she, 'shall split thy heart with sorrow,
> Remember Margaret was a prophetess.' (V,i, 10–27)

6. *Queen Elizabeth and Lady Anne*

Moulton does not include the two women, Queen Elizabeth and Lady Anne, in his discussion of Nemesis and its victims, perhaps because their careers differ somewhat from those of a Clarence or a Hastings. It is true that Queen Elizabeth does not die, while Anne's death, off-stage, is handled so ambiguously as to make it uncertain whether she is murdered or dies of natural causes. It is true, too, that neither woman can be called directly to account for crimes in the way a Buckingham or even a King Edward can. Yet in other respects the two fit the pattern well enough. Each is cursed, for instance, each suffers aptly in terms of the curse, and each comes to recognise the aptness of the suffering she is enduring.

Anne's dramatic career as a victim of Nemesis is distinguished from any other's by the fact that she sets the terms of her own suffering by cursing herself. It is also one of the briefest, since she appears in only two scenes, one of which relates the cause of her suffering and the other its effects.

'Cause' is, indeed, much to the fore in I,ii. Beginning his wooing, Richard asks whether 'The causer of the timeless deaths/ Of these Plantagenets, Henry and Edward,' is not 'As blameful as the executioner?' (I,ii, 117–19). Anne's reply, 'Thou wast the cause of that accursed effect', draws from Richard the typical lover's hyperbole of 'Your beauty was the cause of that effect' (121).

He is, of course, lying, but the exchange sets up an ironic ambiance, reinforced by what follows when Richard tells her that her beauty is his day, his life:

> *Anne*   Black night O'ershade thy day, and death thy life!
> *Gloucester*   Curse not thyself, fair creature; thou art both.
>
> (I,ii, 130–2)

For Anne does curse herself in this scene, albeit unwittingly, when, as part of her lament for the dead Henry VI, she says of Richard:

> If ever he have wife, let her be made
> More miserable by the life of him
> Than I am by my young lord's death and thee! (I,ii, 26–8)

In IV,i, stricken with guilt over the usurpation and her coming coronation, Anne recalls her curse and its ironic outcome:

> O, when, I say, I looked on Richard's face,
> This was my wish: 'Be thou', quoth I, 'accursed,
> For making me, so young, so old a widow!
> And, when thou wed'st, let sorrow haunt thy bed;
> And be thy wife – if any be so – made
> More miserable by the life of thee
> Than thou hast made me by my dear lord's death!'
> Lo, ere I can repeat this curse again,

Within so small a time, my woman's heart
Grossly grew captive to his honey words
And proved the subject of mine own soul's curse,
Which hitherto hath held mine eyes from rest;
For never yet one hour in his bed
Did I enjoy the golden dew of sleep,
But with his timorous dreams was still awaked,
Besides, he hates me for my father Warwick;
And will, no doubt, shortly be rid of me. (IV,i, 71–87)

This account of Anne's sufferings as Richard's wife is interesting not
only for its illustration of the process of retribution as it affects her, but
also for the glimpse it provides into what might be called Richard's
'inner life'. That the outwardly untroubled villain has 'timorous dreams'
is immensely revealing. Like Lady Macbeth, it seems, he can by an effort
of will suppress all pangs of doubt or conscience during his waking hours,
but not when he is asleep. In V,iii we are to observe these 'dreams'
through the medium of the ghosts, and see for ourselves that he is in fact
powerfully affected by 'coward conscience'. Anne's speech prepares us
for that enlarged understanding of Richard's nature.

Though it seems likely that Richard has Anne murdered, this is never
made explicit. She herself fears he will 'shortly be rid of me', and in the
following scene Richard orders that it be given out 'That Anne, my
queen, is sick and like to die' (IV,ii, 55). In IV,iii we are told that 'Anne
my wife hath bid this world good night' (39), and we may wonder
whether, as on other occasions, Richard has given nature a helping hand.
Anne's death is certainly convenient, for it frees 'a jolly thriving wooer'
to seek his niece's hand. Murdered or not, however, she pays most
severely for succumbing to his 'honey words', suffering retribution in a
more brutally ironic fashion, perhaps, than anyone else in the play.

In Queen Elizabeth's case the retributive process is begun with the
curse laid on her by Queen Margaret in I,iii, where the latter prophesies
that Queen Elizabeth will die 'neither mother, wife, nor England's
queen!' (209). Later in the scene Queen Elizabeth attracts Queen
Margaret's attention when she joins Richard in baiting the old Queen.
The latter then adds a prophetic particularity to her earlier curse:

Poor painted queen, vain flourish of my fortune!
Why strew'st thou sugar on that bottled spider,
Whose deadly web ensnareth thee about?
Fool, fool! thou whet'st a knife to kill thyself.
The day will come that thou shalt wish for me
To help thee curse this poisonous bunch-backed toad. (I,iii, 241–6)

Queen Margaret's dire predictions are borne out with their usual
precision. In II,ii King Edward dies, and Queen Elizabeth thereby ceases
to be both wife and queen, while the unmothering is completed by the
Princes' deaths, which she mourns in IV,iv, before acknowledging, in
the face of Queen Margaret's implacable litany of retribution, the
accuracy of the latter's predictions:

O, thou didst prophesy the time would come
That I should wish for thee to help me curse
That bottled spider, that foul bunch-backed toad! (IV,iv, 79–81)

Queen Margaret's celebrated speech, 'I called thee then vain flourish of
my fortune', completes the process of recognition on Queen Elizabeth's
behalf, and this departure from the usual 'speech of recognition' is given
its own peculiar aptness as Queen Margaret symbolically transfers her
rôle, along with its sorrows, to Queen Elizabeth (IV,iv, 109 – 13).

The ambiguous position that Queen Elizabeth occupies for the
remainder of her stage life is exemplified by what follows. The cursing of
Richard, which she shares with the old Duchess of York, is in the vein of
Queen Margaret. But then comes the wooing (by proxy) of the young
Elizabeth, in which her mother stands very much in the place occupied in
I,ii by Anne. This second wooing-scene has frequently been criticized,
and even allowing for the play's patterned formality, might benefit from
cutting in performance, but the parallels with Anne's wooing – the one
persuaded over the corpse of her father-in-law, the other (in a sense) over
the corpses of her sons – bring a piquant irony to the episode; one which
is heightened by our uncertainty as to its outcome. Critical opinion is
very much divided as to whether Queen Elizabeth acquiesces in Richard's
plan to marry his niece or not. Her final comment, 'Write to me very
shortly,/ And you shall understand from me her mind' (IV,iv, 429–30),

is certainly taken by Richard to be agreement. Yet when we hear of Queen Elizabeth for the last time, it is to learn that 'the queen hath heartily consented/ He [Richmond] should espouse Elizabeth her daughter!' (IV,v, 7–8). But whether Queen Elizabeth first agrees to Richard's suit and then changes her mind, or from the first dupes him, there is an irony of which the supreme ironist is quite unconscious in his contemptuous dismissal of her as a 'Relenting fool, and shallow-changing woman!' (IV,iv, 432).

RICHARD

The final Nemesis action involves Richard, and it is tempting to discuss it here, as part of the pattern, for there are significant parallels between Richard's downfall and Clarence's and Buckingham's in particular. Richard is, however, self-evidently a special case, and no examination of his career in terms of retribution alone can adequately convey his significance to the play as a whole. For this reason he must be considered in broader and more comprehensive terms.

Richard as Ideal Villain

It was Moulton who concluded that what marks Richard as an 'ideal' rather than a 'real' villain is the scale and completeness of his wrong-doing, its motivelessness, its effortless artistry, its passionlessness, and its irresistibility.[17] That Richard is a complete villain, with no doubts or hesitations in his commitment to evil, is clear. Moreover, though in his opening soliloquy he offers us motives, based on his deformity, they are more a *donnée* than an adequate explanation for his villainy. For Richard, virtue is never an option, any more than it is, say, for Edmund in *King Lear*. But if virtue is never an option for Richard, nor is failure either, at least until the advent of Richmond. Fortune's wheel and Richard's machinations appear to complement one another perfectly, and his easy artistry seems to be part of the mechanism of history itself.

Yet fruitful as Moulton's ideas are, they need, here, to be supple-

[17]*Shakespeare as Dramatic Artist*, pp.90–103.

mented. For Moulton saw *Richard III* essentially in terms of Nemesis, while this study seeks to show that Nemesis is only part of a patterning of language and action which takes as its ordering principle the idea of history as a pageant. The following approaches to the character of Richard – as humourist, actor-producer, vice, and minister or scourge – are designed to show how crucial to that pageant he is.

Richard as Humourist

Earlier in this study, great stress was laid on the formality of the language in *Richard III*, and in scenes such as the wooing of Anne, Richard was shown to play a significant part in these formal structures. As was then hinted, however, there is another facet of Richard which is quite the reverse of formal, linguistically. Consider, for instance, his parting remarks to the Murderers in I,iii – 'Your eyes drop millstones, when fools' eyes fall tears./ I like you, lads: about your business straight' (I,iii, 353 – 4) – or this exchange with Brakenbury concerning the King's mistress, Jane Shore:

> *Brakenbury* With this, my lord, myself have nought to do.
> *Gloucester* Naught to do with Mistress Shore! I tell thee fellow,
> He that doth naught with her (excepting one)
> Were best to do it secretly, alone. (I,i, 97–100)

In each Richard is conversing with inferiors, but it is not a social factor which occasions this kind of colloquial utterance. In I,i, for instance, we find Gloucester sympathizing with the arrested Clarence:

> Why, this it is, when men are ruled by women:
> 'Tis not the king that sends you to the Tower;
> My Lady Grey his wife, Clarence, 'tis she
> That tempers him to this extremity.
> Was it not she, and that good man of worship,
> Anthony Woodeville, her brother there,
> That made him send Lord Hastings to the Tower,
> From whence this present day he is delivered?
> We are not safe, Clarence, we are not safe. (I,i, 62–70)

The examples could be multiplied, but to no point, for the distinctive features remain the same. Colloquial and jocular, Richard's speech at times like this is in every sense the antithesis of the formality so widespread in the play. More will be said shortly about the underlying implications of this informality. Here the point at issue is the bifold effect that it has on our conception of Richard and of the play.

In the first place, this informality and humour sets Richard apart from the remainder of the characters. Buckingham may occasionally share a joke with his master, or Catesby echo him, but nonetheless there is a gulf fixed between Richard and the rest – between the humourist and the raw material for his humour. This places Richard outside the pageant, so to speak, in a way unmatched even by Queen Margaret. Yet at the same time the kind of humour in which he indulges, ironic and frequently mocking, serves to link him to the audience. Enjoying such black humour as is evidenced in

> I'll marry Warwick's youngest daughter.
> What though I killed her husband and her father?
> The readiest way to make the wench amends
> Is to become her husband and her father (I,i, 153–6)

we become, in a sense, accomplices of Richard's, suspending our moral judgements in the enjoyment of his villainy. Irony relies on a gap between the spoken and the unspoken. Richard and the audience are on one side of that gap, and the remainder of the cast on the other.

Richard as Actor – Producer

Richard is not only a humourist but also an actor, and by this, too, he is set apart from the rest of the *dramatis personae*. A consummate performer, he varies his rôle according to the audience within the play, and deals straightforwardly only with us and, for brief moments, with Buckingham and with underlings like Tyrrel or the Murderers. We know, because he tells us so, that he is plotting Clarence's death, but to his unsuspecting brother he is all gentle solicitude when he asks, 'But what's the matter, Clarence? may I know?' (I,i, 51). We know, too, that he intends marrying Anne as an instrument of policy, yet to her he appears the very image of the prostrate lover, full of clichés in his justification of the murders he has undertaken (I,ii, 121 – 4).

And so it goes on. Bawdily punning with Brakenbury and Clarence (I,i, 97), he yet evinces with a Bishop on either arm a puritanical horror of swearing (III,vii, 220). Equally piously, he manages to outdo everyone else in the reconciliation engineered by King Edward in saying:

> I do not know that Englishman alive
> With whom my soul is any jot at odds
> More than the infant that is born to-night:
> I thank my God for my humility. (II,i, 70–3)

Yet in the next instant again, he is reacting with beautifully simulated surprise and anger to Queen Elizabeth's innocent mention of Clarence and preparing the ground for the alliance with Hastings and Buckingham which will destroy her and her kinsmen.

Joined by Buckingham, Richard achieves his greatest success in producing and starring in the comedy of the usurpation (III,v, and vii). Opening, ironically enough, with a discussion between Richard and Buckingham about the feigning of the tragic emotions (III,v, 1–11), the 'play' turns out to be a frequently farcical performance, grossly over-acted but withal finely suited to the gullibility of the Mayor and Citizens (III,vii, 95 – 103).

Characteristically full of ironies, perceived or engineered by Richard and shared with us, the usurpation marks the high point in his career as an actor and producer. It is, indeed, his last success, save the hollow one involved in wooing Queen Elizabeth. When the upward movement of his career is halted, and the downward turn begins, there is neither time for further acting, nor opportunity.

Richard as Vice

When, in I,iii, Buckingham rejects Queen Margaret's warning against consorting with Richard, she retorts, 'What, dost thou scorn me for my gentle counsel?/ And soothe the devil that I warn thee from?' (297–8). In isolation, the remark might be dismissed as prophetic hyperbole. But the identification of Richard with the devil is not an isolated one, nor restricted to statements by his enemies. When, for instance, Queen Elizabeth parries Richard's blandishments with 'Shall I be tempted of the devil thus?', he himself replies, 'Ay, if the devil tempt you to do good' (IV,iv, 419–20). And elsewhere he makes more explicit statements about his devilry. In I,iii, for example, he lists the villainies he is engaged in and then adds, with evident delight:

> But then I sigh; and, with a piece of Scripture,
> Tell them that God bids us do good for evil:
> And thus I clothe my naked villany
> With odd old ends stol'n forth of Holy Writ;
> And seem a saint, when most I play the devil. (334–8)

While in III,i the most significant statement of all not only reinforces this sense of the devilish in Richard, but also relates it tellingly to aspects of his personality already discussed:

> Thus, like the formal Vice, Iniquity,
> I moralize two meanings in one word. (III,i, 82–3)

A traditional figure in the medieval morality play, the Vice was at once a destructive agent and a kind of clown, a cynical villain and a grim humourist who mocked virtue and, taking advantage of his ambiguous position half inside and half outside the dramatic action, invited us to share his enjoyment of evil rather than condemn it.

The substantial identity between Richard's rôle and that of the Vice is unmistakeable. Beguiling us with his confidences, as he has done since the opening soliloquy, Richard here not only reveals a fundamental aspect of his character but on Shakespeare's behalf, as it were, gives us an important new insight into the dramatic strategy around which *Richard III* is constructed.

Richard as Minister and Scourge

Richard's identification with the Vice provides a satisfying rationale for his various traits of character – his black humour, his delight in acting, and above all his total commitment to villainy. Moreover, as Iniquity Richard possesses a traditional dramatic warrant for his anomalous stance, at once part of and separate from the main dramatic action; a stance which greatly reinforces the sense of the 'frantic play' within the play.

There remains, however, one further dimension – a paradoxical one – which requires elucidation. The paradox is revealed succinctly by Queen Margaret, who in IV,iv talks of a 'hell-hound that doth hunt us all to death' (48) and a 'foul defacer of God's handiwork' (51), yet also thanks God for the activities of 'this carnal cur' (56). The paradox is intensified by Margaret's next speech, in which she catalogues Richard's victims and adds:

> Richard yet lives, hell's black intelligencer,
> Only reserved their factor, to buy souls
> And send them thither: (71–3)

To resolve this paradox, whereby Richard is seen as an agent of Hell, yet God is thanked for his activities, we need to understand the traditional Christian concepts of the Minister and the Scourge, and their relationship to Providence.

Writing of 'Hamlet as Minister and Scourge', Fredson Bowers sums up the essential distinction between the two by remarking that 'a minister of God, in contrast to a scourge, is an agent who directly performs some good'.[18] He goes on, however, to add this important qualification:

> A retributive minister may visit God's wrath on sin but only as the final act to the overthrow of evil, whereas a scourge visits wrath alone, the delayed good to rest in another's hands.[19]

The application to *Richard III* is clear, and Bowers himself notes it. Richard is the classic scourge, 'the final agent of God's vengeance for the deposition and murder of the anointed Richard II', while Richmond is the 'minister who will bring to a close God's wrath by exacting public justice in battle'.[20]

As will be seen, the view of the minister and scourge as essentially

[18]*P.M.L.A.* LXX (1955), pp.743 – 4.
[19]*Ibid.*, p.744.
[20]*Ibid.*, p.744.

complementary implies that in some manner God can direct the forces of evil to good ends. This, indeed, Shakespeare's contemporaries believed, seeing God's providential hand even in the fall of the sparrow. As one Elizabethan bishop put it:

> Thus must we in all things that be done, whether they be good or evil (except sin, which God hates and causes not), not only look at the second causes, which be but God's means and instruments whereby he works, but have a further eye, and look up to God.[21]

There remains, though, a paradox. How can the Devil (or a Richard acting so enthusiastically on his behalf) be made a positive contributor to the Divine purpose? In a passage of some subtlety, John Calvin supplies what was, to the Elizabethans at least, a convincing answer:

> Now when we say that Satan resisteth God, that the works of Satan disagree with the works of God, we doo therewithall affirme that this disagreement and strife hangeth vpon the sufferance of God. I speake not now of his will, nor of his endeuor, but of the effect onely. For sith the diuell is wicked of nature, he is not inclined to obey the will of God, but is wholly caried to stubbornesse and rebellion. This therefore he hath of himselfe and of his owne wickednesse, that of desire and purpose he withstandeth God. And by this wickednesse he is stirred vp to the enterprising of those things that he knoweth to be most against God. But because God holdeth him fast tied and restrained with the bridle of his power, he executeth onely those things that are granted him from God. And so doth he obey his creator whether he will or no, because he is constrained to applie his seruice whither soeuer God compelleth him.[22]

The result is the ultimate futility of evil in its ironic involvement as an agent for good. Richard may be totally committed to villainy and (until the advent of Richmond) immensely successful, but in a sense his activity is pointless. For when the scourge has done his work, and the retributive process is in other respects complete, he must himself fall victim to God's minister. Being so immensely efficient himself, Richard merely hastens

[21]James Pilkington, *Works*, ed. J.Scholefield (1853), p.227.
[22]*The Institution of Christian Religion*, trans. Thomas Norton (1611), pp.70 – 1.

his own end. And for that, Queen Margaret may well give thanks.

The Decline of Richard

It is easy to assume, looking at the ideal villain of *3 Henry VI* and *Richard III*, that Richard is a stereotypic figure in whom no personality change takes place. This is not so. Until the end of IV, i his personality is as predictable as his success. From IV, ii onwards, however, neither is certain. He secures a few further successes – e.g. ridding himself of the princes, wooing Queen Anne, and despatching Buckingham – though each is of uncertain value. Equally, though he displays at times his old coolness and zest, his nerve and his judgement are increasingly fallible. The alienation of Buckingham is a failure of judgement. Another, more telling, lapse, however, is that in IV,iv, where Richard is sufficiently flustered to give incomplete and contradictory instructions to Ratcliffe and Catesby and to strike the Messenger bearing (as Richard thinks) further bad news.

The series of events reported to Richard in the latter part of IV,iv represents a considerable compression of historical time on Shakespeare's part. This dramatic shorthand is extremely effective, however, in conveying the pressure exerted on Richard. Good, bad, or (sometimes) good and bad perplexingly intermingled, the incessant communiques never give him time to take stock, and by the time we meet him at Bosworth, he is far from the ebullient figure he was, uncharacteristically introspective and subdued in his momentary speculation about death, 'Up with my tent! Here will I lie to-night - / But where to-morrow?' (V,iii, 7 – 8) and his call for wine (73 – 5). It is in this dark frame of mind that Richard is visited (like Richmond, sleeping the sleep of the just near by) by the ghosts of his many victims. In Shakespeare's plays the precise nature of ghosts, morally and theologically, can be a matter of lively debate. In *Richard III*, however, there is no reason to doubt their objective existence (as in *Macbeth*) or their moral standing (as in *Hamlet*). In visiting Richmond as well as Richard, and bringing cheer as well as condemnation, they are a visible summation of the retributive process now nearing its end and an earnest of the peace to come.

Thoroughly unnerved by his 'dream', Richard reveals the full extent of the changes wrought in him in the agonized contradictions of his self-examination:

> O coward conscience, how dost thou afflict me!
> The lights burn blue. It is now dead midnight.
> Cold fearful drops stand on my trembling flesh.
> What do I fear? myself? there's none else by.
> Richard loves Richard; that is, I am I.
> Is there a murderer here? No — yes, I am:
> Then fly. What, from myself? Great reason why —
> Lest I revenge. Myself upon myself?
> Alack, I love myself. For any good
> That I myself have done unto myself?
> O, no! Alas, I rather hate myself
> For hateful deeds committed by myself!
> I am a villain: yet I lie, I am not.
> Fool, of thyself speak well: fool, do not flatter.
> My conscience hath a thousand several tongues,
> And every tongue brings in a several tale,
> And every tale condemns me for a villain.
> Perjury, perjury, in the high'st degree;
> Murder, stern murder, in the dir'st degree;
> All several sins, all used in each degree,
> Throng to the bar, crying all 'Guilty! guilty!'. (179 – 99)

The process by which Richard reaches this point of disintegration has been well documented by William B. Toole, who demonstrates that the theme of division within the play, which in macrocosm is manifested in social and political terms, is evident microcosmically in Richard himself.[23] From the first, Richard presents two images of himself. The public image (the 'shadow', to use a metaphor of which Richard himself is fond) is that of the straightforward man of conscience; the private that of the dedicated villain. Through his intelligence and will, Richard maintains the twin images until IV, ii. Then the pressure grows and the fundamental division within his personality emerges, to be most fully expressed

[23]'The Motif of Psychic Division in *Richard III*', *Shakespeare Survey*, 27 (1974) pp.21 – 32.

under the pressure of the 'shadows' whom Richard finds more terrifying than 'the substance of ten thousand soldiers/ ... led by shallow Richmond' (218 – 19). Despairing and afraid, he dies in battle, unhistorically slain by Richmond. Though God's minister may take the credit, however, the fact is that Richard has more or less destroyed himself, and in battle seems, like Macbeth at bay, a shell of a man, sustained only by a survival reflex.

RICHMOND

It was remarked earlier that the decline of Richard's fortunes and the disintegration of his personality dates from that moment when Stanley observes that 'Dorset ... is fled/ To Richmond'. Though we do not meet Richmond himself until V, ii, and then only briefly, his name, frequently mentioned in reports, keeps the threat to Richard constantly before us. Not only that, but Richard's own preoccupation with Richmond in IV, ii and iv, his sense that the latter represents the only threat worth worrying about and that two prophecies – Henry VI's and the Irish bard's – reinforce that feeling, serves to make us feel that in Richmond lies Richard's doom.

Having become so conscious of Richmond's importance, however, we are likely to be disappointed when we finally meet the man. Richmond speaks only 20 lines in his important first appearance, in V,ii, and these give us no real sense of the individual. Whether expressing a pious trust in God or denouncing the 'wretched, bloody, and usurping boar', he says the expected, but no more. The focus in the scene in fact is strongly on Richard and his predicament as a 'guilty homicide', and not upon Richmond at all.

It is much the same in the tableau-like scene which follows. With Richard's tent on one side of the stage and Richmond's on the other, V,iii maintains a strict alternation of focus between the two camps. Yet for all this patterned even-handedness, to which even the ghosts are party, interest is never evenly divided between the two men. Richmond's peace of mind is morally appropriate but dramatically uninteresting, while his oration to his troops says the expected in colourless terms. Richard's speech to his troops, on the other hand, is a lively if scurrilous diatribe which shows much of the zest of the earlier Richard, while the insights we are given into his thoughts and feelings elsewhere in the scene show us how great an effort is required to summon up that zest.

Nor does the final scene establish Richmond any more individually. His one big speech says exactly what is needed about peace and reconciliation, but behind the words the man is insubstantial:

> England hath long been mad, and scarred herself;
> The brother blindly shed the brother's blood,
> The father rashly slaughtered his own son,
> The son, compelled, been butcher to the sire:
> All that divided York and Lancaster
> Divided in their dire division,
> O, now let Richmond and Elizabeth,
> The true succeeders of each royal house,
> By God's fair ordinance conjoin together! (V,v, 23 – 31)

If we compare this to Richard's opening soliloquy (and the general tendency to pattern and various verbal parallels and echoes suggest that a comparison is intended) we can see the limitations of Richmond's last speech with great clarity. Both speeches are admirable thematically, but only Richard's is particularized. Any pious prince could utter Richmond's speech in V,v. Richard's in I,i is his alone.

RICHARD, RICHMOND, AND QUEEN MARGARET

There can be little doubt that Shakespeare deliberately circumscribed his portrayal of Richmond, making him thematically adequate as an impeccably orthodox (and conscious) instrument of providence, but denying him such individualizing traits as might make him a rival of Richard's in dramatic terms. The anonymous author of *The True Tragedy*, by contrast, builds up the character of Richmond so that he eventually supplants Richard dramatically as well as historically.

These different approaches not only represent alternative dramatic strategies for concluding the story of Richard III, but also imply differing assessments of the importance of the thematic material. *The True Tragedy* ends with an unequivocal emphasis on the kinds of issues that are central, e.g., to Hall's moral history. With the coming of the Tudor deliverer, peace is restored and the bloody past forgotten. To this end we are treated not only to a formal betrothal scene involving Richmond and Princess Elizabeth, but also to a panegyric directed at the glorious inheritor of all the Tudor virtues, Queen Elizabeth herself. In *Richard III*, on the other hand, Shakespeare treads a subtler path, not neglecting the thematic concerns inherited from Hall or Holinshed, but subordinating them to an artistic conception of the play closer to More than to Hall, and having as its focus the concept of history as a pageant and the richly complementary notion of Richard as ideal villain, standing, Vice-like, between us and that pageant.

This approach to his material involves Shakespeare in a highly delicate balancing act. One aspect of this has already been observed in the Richmond scenes, where Shakespeare is at pains to protect the dramatic stature of his villainous hero without undermining the thematic issues. Another aspect, perhaps even more instructive, is seen in the relationship of Richard and Queen Margaret. In his adaptation of *Richard III*, first performed in 1700 and more or less exclusively preferred on the English stage until the late nineteenth century, Colley Cibber almost entirely excised the character of the old Queen – as indeed he totally excised those of King Edward, Clarence, and Hastings. These cuts were made to maximize the impact of Richard, but the cost – albeit unrecognized by Cibber – was enormous. For Queen Margaret's place in the play is second in importance only to Richard's, and her sense both of the nature and meaning of events and of their shape is crucial to our experience of the dramatic action. Without it, *Richard III* is much diminished – and not just in length.

But it is not only we who lose if *Richard III* is taken, as by Cibber and (in a sense) by Olivier in the film, to be primarily a vehicle for Richard, but also Richard himself. For his virtuosity in villainy to be more than mere virtuosity, he requires the context of moral history – and its inhabitants – within which to operate. As Nicholas Brooke so neatly puts it, 'the play, once deprived of its moral history, was deprived of any adequate opposition to Richard; so that his stature, which Cibber might

seem to have enhanced, was in fact diminished'.[24] By way of illustrating
Brooke's point, and demonstrating the nature and validity of Shakespeare's balancing act, we might consider here the confrontation between
Margaret and Richard in I,iii. The scene derives its tension from the fact
that the conflict is between Richard and the only character capable of
meeting on anything like equal terms his intelligence and strength of
will. From the first exchange, when Richard's 'Foul wrinkléd witch,
what mak'st thou in my sight?' is met with 'But repetition of what thou
hast marred;/ That will I make before I let thee go' (164–6), Margaret
steadfastly withstands his pressure as he withstands hers. He gains an
advantage when he recalls the death of 'pretty Rutland' and thereby
unites the others against her, but she regains the ascendancy when she
curses Edward IV, the Queen, Rivers, Dorset, and Hastings (195–214).
Richard interrupts her with 'Have done thy charm, thou hateful
withered hag!', but her response is to turn on him with intensified
venom:

> And leave out thee? stay, dog, for thou shalt hear me.
> If heaven have any grievous plague in store
> Exceeding those that I can wish upon thee,
> O, let them keep it till thy sins be ripe,
> And then hurl down their indignation
> On thee, the troubler of the poor world's peace! (I,iii, 216 – 21)

As her curse gives way to vituperation, Richard regains the initiative
with a piece of schoolboy effrontery, slipping her name in ahead of his
own to turn the curse back on her (232 – 9). Here again he succeeds in
uniting the others against her, but as before she meets their jibes with a
ferocity which only Richard can counter and even he cannot suppress
(273 – 8).

Overall, the battle is inconclusive, with victory to neither side. It is
worth noting, though, that it is only after Margaret has left that Richard
can resume his ascendancy over those around him. While Margaret is
present, his customary pious and charitable pose is impossible.

I,iii illustrates neatly the importance of the challenge to Richard that

[24]*Shakespeare's Early Tragedies* (1968), p.49.

Margaret represents, and the loss that must be incurred if she is, as by Cibber, to be all but removed from the play. We can also see, by contrast, how completely Richmond fails to provide such a challenge to Richard's dramatic supremacy, and how sure Shakespeare's touch is in ensuring that he cannot do this. Richmond may inherit the kingdom of England, and blessed peace come again thereby, but in dramatic terms Richard must not be deposed, though the exigencies of history demand that in the end he be destroyed.

THE CITIZEN CHORUS

In certain respects, *Richard III* provides plenty of opportunity for the balancing provided by choric comment. For though all the major characters save two are caught up in the 'frantic play', each victim of Richard's has, prior to death, a moment of recognition in which he sets his life and death in perspective. Moreover, both Richard and Margaret, who to more or less degree stand outside the 'play', are acutely aware of what they are doing and how it relates to that inner structure, and Richard, at least, comments directly to us about it.

Yet for all this, there is very little which gives a truly independent perspective on characters and events — i.e. a view of them free of the bias conferred by participation. The two notable exceptions are the scenes which involve the ordinary man — the three citizens in II,iii and the Scrivener in III,vi.

II,iii is a choric scene which in the light of similar scenes in later Shakespearean plays, like *Richard II*, may seem less remarkable than in fact it was for its time. Compared to contemporary choric methods, which mainly took the form of formal reflective utterances put in the mouths of leading characters, II,iii is unusually informal. The three Citizens meet casually as they go about their business, and discuss, in passing, the affairs of the day and their implications. What is more, their conversation reveals three different reactions to events at court mirrored in three different personalities:

> 3 Citizen   Doth the news hold of good King Edward's death?
> 2 Citizen   Ay, sir, it is too true, God help the while!

> *3 Citizen*   Then, masters, look to see a troublous world.
> *1 Citizen*   No, no; by God's good grace his son shall reign.
> *3 Citizen*   Woe to that land that's governed by a child!
> *2 Citizen*   In him there is a hope of government,
> Which, in his nonage, council under him,
> And, in his full and ripened years, himself,
> No doubt, shall then, and till then, govern well.
> *1 Citizen*   So stood the state when Henry the Sixth
> Was crowned in Paris but at nine months old.
> *3 Citizen*   Stood the state so? No, no, good friends, God wot;
> For then this land was famously enriched
> With politic grave counsel; then the king
> Had virtuous uncles to protect his grace. (II,iii, 7–21)

The First Citizen is clearly unsophisticated, with his simplistic comparison of Henry VI's minority and Edward V's. The Third Citizen, however, is a shrewd and well-informed commentator whose awareness of the dissension likely among the young King's uncles, paternal and maternal, and of the danger posed by Richard, is followed by an impressive general statement whose insight is underlined by the corroborative statement from the Second Citizen:

> *3 Citizen*   When clouds are seen, wise men put on their cloaks;
> When great leaves fall, then winter is at hand;
> When the sun sets, who doth not look for night?
> Untimely storms makes men expect a dearth.
> All may be well; but, if God sort it so,
> 'Tis more than we deserve, or I expect.
> *2 Citizen*   Truly, the hearts of men are full of fear:
> You cannot reason almost with a man
> That looks not heavily and full of dread. (II,iii, 32–40)

The combination here of pithy apophthegms and richly allusive metaphors conveys an air of foreboding all the stronger for the fact that it is being expressed by ordinary men in ordinary terms. The pageant that takes up the bulk of the dramatic action is of necessity entirely self-contained and remote from the day-to-day lives of the citizens. What is made clear here, however, is that its effects are felt even at the most humble social level.

The second of the scenes involving choric comment from the citizenry is III,vi. Like the three Citizens, the Scrivener is an anonymous figure, but like them he is of considerable importance as an 'outside' voice, reflecting general concern at what is happening. In the preceding scene the Mayor, totally deceived by the performance of Richard and Buckingham, had given his assent to the death of Hastings (III,v, 46 – 8). Now, however, the Scrivener makes clear his awareness of the trumped-up nature of Hastings' execution:

> Here is the indictment of the good Lord Hastings,
> Which in a set hand fairly is engrossed,
> That it may be to-day read o'er in Paul's.
> And mark how well the sequel hangs together:
> Eleven hours I have spent to write it over,
> For yesternight by Catesby was it sent me;
> The precedent was full as long a-doing:
> And yet within these five hours Hastings lived,
> Untainted, unexamined, free, at liberty. (III,vi, 1–9)

Coming as it does between two scenes in which the schemes of Richard and Buckingham are in full swing, this comment is highly effective. Linked to the report of the silent disapproval with which the citizens received Buckingham's speech in favour of Richard's assumption to the throne (III,vii, 1–43), it indicates that while their Mayor and leading notables might be duped, the citizens in general are not.

Like II,iii, III,vi concludes with remarks which broaden the perspective from the particular to the general:

> Here's a good world the while! Who is so gross,
> That cannot see this palpable device?
> Yet who's so bold, but says he sees it not?
> Bad is the world; and all will come to nought,
> When such ill dealing must be seen in thought. (III,vi, 10–14)

The three Citizens concluded that man should 'leave it all to God' (II,iii, 45). The Scrivener is convinced that 'all will come to nought'. Together the two remarks sum up the play's outcome neatly. God will provide a deliverer (in Richmond) and Richard's schemes will fail. We have this on good choric authority, long before Richard's fortunes begin to decline, or Richmond is first mentioned. It is a significant corrective to Richard's beguiling villainy and seemingly endless run of brilliant successes.

IRONY AND DISTANCE

That *Richard III* is suffused throughout with irony needs little arguing. Nor is there any doubt that of all the sources of irony in the play, the greatest is Richard himself. Whether thanking God for his 'humility' or blasphemously joking about the 'butt-end of a mother's blessing', assuring King Edward that 't'is death to me to be at emnity' or grossly flattering Buckingham with 'My other self, my counsel's consistory,/ My oracle, my prophet, my dear cousin!', Richard not only delights in the ironies he finds all about him, but induces us to share that delight with him. And because almost all of his ironic perceptions involve his villainy, he in a sense makes accomplices of us, inducing us to set aside our customary moral scruples in the enjoyment of such witticisms as 'Simple, plain Clarence, I do love thee so,/ That I will shortly send thy soul to heaven,' (I,i, 118 – 19).

This collaboration in the recognition and enjoyment of ironies depends on two factors. The first is the absence of any identification with the victims of Richard's villainy. So long as they are seen by us as merely actors in the 'frantic play' and demand no empathy on our part, there is no difficulty. Hence a Clarence, a Hastings, or a Buckingham, can be a fertile source of ironic amusement. When, however, Richard has the Princes murdered in the Tower, the tone changes, and instead of a lightly ironic, distanced comment, we get the following from Tyrrel:

> The tyrannous and bloody act is done,
> The most arch deed of piteous massacre
> That ever yet this land was guilty of.
> Dighton and Forrest, whom I did suborn
> To do this piece of ruthless butchery,
> Albeit they were fleshed villains, bloody dogs,

Melting with tenderness and mild compassion,
Wept like two children in their death's sad story.
'O, thus,' quoth Dighton, 'lay the gentle babes':
'Thus, thus,' quoth Forrest, 'girdling one another
Within their alabaster innocent arms:
Their lips were four red roses on a stalk,
Which in their summer beauty kissed each other. (IV,iii, 1 – 13)

Just as the unbroken run of Richard's successes ends with the first
mention of Richmond, so the unbroken collaboration between Richard
and us ends with the murder of the Princes. Though we can thereafter
laugh with Richard, we do so intermittently, and with an increasing
moral unease, an unease heightened by the sense we have of Richard's
growing fallibility. For the second factor encouraging our collaboration
with Richard is, to quote Moulton's phrase, the 'fascination of his irresistibility'. His irresistibility is part of Richard's ideal villainy, and that
sense of the ideal in part licences our collaboration with him. But once he
begins to falter, we no longer feel obliged to suspend judgement.

The last part of the play, therefore, involves a gradual process of with-
drawal on our part from association with Richard. This process is not
accompanied by a concomitant developing association with Richmond,
which Shakespeare clearly prevents. Nor is it an entirely straightforward
process. There are times when the old, zestful Richard elicits from us the
old, zestful response, as for instance, in his exchange with the circum-
locutious Stanley (IV,iv, 457 – 63). We can even respond with something like the old enjoyment when, having rid himself of his wife,
Richard proclaims himself a 'jolly thriving wooer' (IV,iii, 43).

It should be noted, however, that not even during these moments is
the old nexus re-established. Our response is to the vigorous collo-
quialisms rather than to any ironies they express. Indeed, from IV,ii
onwards, Richard is in no position to generate and point out ironies as he
formerly did. That rôle depended on his capacity to control events and
manipulate his opponents. When that capacity is lost, then Richard's
ironic capacity is lost also. In the last phase of his dramatic existence, he
becomes, if anything, the object of ironies rather than the creator of
them, and our emancipation from him is thereby completed.

4. Conclusions

This study of *Richard III* has argued a view of the play as balancing moral history and ideal villainy through the device of the 'pageant', the 'frantic play' within the play. Like Nicholas Brooke, I am convinced that the two elements — moral history and ideal villainy — are interdependent, 'and that the contrast between them is ... an important structural device, elaborated to its maximum effect in the use of contrasting linguistic and dramatic modes'.[25] Brooke concludes that the outcome of this contrast 'can properly be called tragic'. His thesis is that the play shows the destruction of the individual human will by the 'gigantic machine' of order, manifested in retributive history, and that there is a sense in which Richard, who 'derived his rôle from the Vice of the Moralities',

> becomes in the end Mankind as well (though not, of course, Everyman): the human representative, bolder than ourselves, resisting oppression and being destroyed.[26]

This is not the place to argue the merits of the 'divine pattern' (which Brooke finds 'repulsive'), or the niceties of the theological schema which underlies it (of which something was said earlier). It is, however, worth noting the dramatic conclusion that Brooke comes to vis-à-vis Richard; namely that 'the world not only seems, but is, the poorer for his loss'. This the dramatic experience itself seems to contradict. With a Hamlet, a Macbeth, or even a Romeo we can speak of a sense of loss because we can identify unfulfilled promise. In Richard, however, all that his personality promises is abundantly fulfilled. He is 'determinéd to prove a villain', and does it brilliantly, bringing all his talents to bear on the task. To ask more by speaking of 'loss' is akin to asking more of a Falstaff or any great comic villain. For indeed it is in comparison with such comic figures that

[25]*Shakespeare's Early Tragedies*, pp.49–50.
[26]*Ibid.*, p.79.

Richard and his villainous energies can best be measured. Nor is it, perhaps, entirely coincidence that when the second tetralogy came to be written, Shakespeare wrote increasingly in the vein of comic history. In *The Tragedy of Richard the Third*, we have a work which is much more a precursor of *Henry IV* than of *Richard II*, and, with its consciously 'dramatic' structure and 'ideal' central figure, much closer to *Henry V* than to either.

Further Reading

There are, as with all Shakespeare's plays, a myriad of editions of *Richard III* which might be consulted. One of the most reliable collected editions of Shakespeare is that by Peter Alexander (1951), while amongst separate editions of *Richard III* those by John Dover-Wilson in the New Shakespeare Series (1965) and E.A.J. Honigmann in the New Penguin Shakespeare (1968) both offer scholarly but accessible annotation and reliable texts.

The following books are amongst those which have contributed substantially to the understanding of *Richard III*.

Nicholas Brooke, *Shakespeare's Early Tragedies* (1968).

Geoffrey Bullough, *Narrative and Dramatic Sources of Shakespeare*, III (1960).

Wolfgang Clemen, *A Commentary on Shakespeare's Richard III* (1968).

R.G. Moulton, *Shakespeare as a Dramatic Artist* (1888).

A.P. Rossiter, *Angel With Horns* (1961).

E.M.W. Tillyard, *Shakespeare's History Plays* (1944).

W.B. Toole, 'The Motif of Psychic Division in *Richard III*', *Shakespeare Survey*, 27 (1974).

Derek Traversi, *An Approach to Shakespeare*. Vol.1: *Henry VI to Twelfth Night* (1968).

Index